Great Christian Prayers
Their history and meaning

Stephen Redmond SJ

Throughout a history of two thousands years, Christians have proclaimed the Christ-event and Christ's continuing presence among us through prayer. This book presents a cross section of the greatest of these prayers along with simple and accessible historical and theological notes which help to bring out their full significance and meaning for today's Christians. For ease of use, the prayers are given with the relevant notes on the facing pages.

The collection starts with the prayers of the New Testament and moves on to some great Alleluia prayers of praise, prayers focusing on Jesus, a celebration of the Holy Spirit and prayers in praise of Our Lady. 'Signed and Last Prayers' is a journey through the centuries from Augustine of Africa to Baudouin of the Belgians and 'The Sign and the Signature' recalls the be-all and end-all of Christian Prayer. Fr Redmond ends the book with a selection of musical settings for some of the prayers.

Fr Stephen Redmond, an Irish Jesuit, taught for many years in Gonzaga College, Dublin and was on the staff of the Jesuit Novitiate in Lusaka. He is author of *Christ is Your Life, The Mass Through Time, Prayers of Two Peoples* and *The Music of the Gospel.*

STEPHEN REDMOND SJ

GREAT
CHRISTIAN
PRAYERS

THEIR HISTORY AND MEANING

THE COLUMBA PRESS
DUBLIN 2001

THE COLUMBA PRESS
55A Spruce Avenue, Stillorgan Industrial Park,
Blackrock, Co Dublin

First edition 2001
Designed by Bill Bolger
Reproduction of *The Annunciation* by Jacques Yverni, courtesy
of the National Gallery of Ireland.
Origination by
The Columba Press
Printed in Ireland by
Colour Books Ltd, Dublin

ISBN 1 85607 325 4

Acknowledgements:
Much of this book appeared in article form in *The Pioneer.*
My thanks to the editor of that magazine for facilitating re-
publication. Thanks too to Veritas Publications for agreeing to
the re-appearance of three pieces of mine which they pub-
lished in *Prayers of Two Peoples*, and to F.I.A.T. Publications
for prayer 2 on page 89 from *Baudouin, King of the Belgians,*
by Cardinal Suenens.

CONTENTS

*In tribute
to my friends in the faith
living and departed*

.

PREFACE

Christianity is a fact of human history: a towering fact over two millennia. And an indispensable fact of the Christian reality is prayer. In this book I make some attempt to link Christian history and Christian prayer. Prayer of course is done by persons; so to a large extent the book is a portrait gallery of the named and nameless, of individuals and communities of various cultures, characteristics and spiritual states, all united in faith in Christ.

I hope that the book will enhance readers' appreciation of this rich heritage and deepen their own practice of prayer. May our prayer include thanksgiving that we are members of a people that prays in intimate union with Christ: 'he prays for us as our priest, he prays in us as our head, he is prayed to by us as our God' (Saint Augustine).

Stephen Redmond SJ

Many of the prayers in this book are translations from Latin or Irish in whole or in part by Stephen Redmond. The major translations are denoted by asterisks (**).

Christian prayer begins with Jesus himself. His prayer was an important expression of his human one-ness with us. The gospels frequently show him praying and here and there give us the texts of his prayers.

All these texts, except one of those from the Cross, are addressed to the 'Father'. Mark gives us the actual word used by Jesus in Gethsemane: the Aramaic 'Abba', from the main vernacular of Palestine at the time. Aramaic-speaking children addressed their father as 'Abba'; it was a word of intimacy, love, trust, respect. We can safely say that the prayers of Jesus were 'Abba' prayers, that he taught his disciples to pray this way and that 'Abba' praying quickly became Christian practice (see Rom 8:15-16; Gal 4:6).

1. 'I thank thee, Father…' Jesus thanks the Abba that 'the little ones' have by the Father's grace been responsive to his (Jesus') teaching – in contrast to his opponents in the religious establishment who think they have nothing to learn. In Aramaic the text has a three-beat poetic pattern used by him for specially important statements.

2. 'Father, I thank thee…' This is his prayer before he raises Lazarus. It is a reminder of his union with the Father and of his intercession for us (see Heb 7:25).

3. This prayer concludes a few lines in which Jesus speaks of his anguish of heart in the face of his imminent Passion: the passage is the counterpart in John to the Gethsemane agony in the other gospels. The prayer is an acceptance of the Passion as part of the showing-forth of the divine glory and power.

1. THE PRAYERS OF THE NEW TESTAMENT

THE PRAYERS OF JESUS

1. I thank you, Father, Lord of heaven and earth, because you have hidden these things from the wise and the intelligent and have revealed them to infants; yes, Father, for such was your gracious will. (Mt 11:25-26; Lk 10:21)

2. Father, I thank you for having heard me. I knew that you always hear me, but I have said this for the sake of the crowd standing here, so that they may believe that you sent me. (Jn 11:41-42)

3. Father, glorify your name. (Jn 12:28)

John ends his Supper-room sequence with a special high-light of his gospel: the high-priestly prayer of Jesus. This is by far the longest prayer of Jesus in the gospels, echo-ing the Our Father in Matthew and Luke and the pro-logue in John and summing up the mission of the Lord. In its serene hymnal style it contrasts with the prayers of the Passion. It is very much an 'Abba' prayer: 'Father' occurs six times as a kind of refrain. It may have accompanied the institution of the Eucharist.

Jesus celebrates the redemptive mission of the Father and the Son. He praises his disciples for their faith and intercedes for them with great tenderness that they may be 'one' (literally, 'one thing'), protected from 'the evil one' and 'sanctified in truth'.

He prays for his Church, for all who will ever believe in him. The key-word is 'one' ('one thing'): it occurs four times in three consecutive verses. He prays for a unity among Christians that is modelled on and is a sharing in the mutual love of Father and Son; a unity to be the great sign in the world of them both and to be perfected in eter-nal life.

This prayer is one of the great treasures of Christian faith. It is a song of love from the Heart of Christ.

THE PRAYERS OF JESUS

Father, the hour has come; glorify your Son that the Son may glorify you, since you have given him authority over all people, to give eternal life to all whom you have given him… I glorified you on earth, having accomplished the work which you gave me to do; and now, Father, glorify me with the glory which I had with you before the world was made.

I have made your name known to those whom you gave me from the world. They were yours, and you gave them to me, and they have kept your word. Now they know that everything that you have given me is from you; for the words that you gave to me I have given to them, and they have received them and know in truth that I came from you; and they have believed that you sent me.

I am asking on their behalf; I am not asking on behalf of the world but on behalf of those whom you gave me, because they are yours. All mine are yours, and yours are mine, and I have been glorified in them. And now I am no longer in the world, but they are in the world, and I am coming to you. Holy Father, protect them in your name that you have given me, so that they may be one, as we are one. While I was with them, I protected them in your name that you have given me: I guarded them, and not one of them was lost except the one destined to be lost, so that the scripture might be fulfilled.

But now I am coming to you; and I speak these things in the world, so that they may have my joy made complete in themselves. I have given them your word; and the world has hated them because they do not belong to the world, just as I do not belong to the world. I am not asking you to take them out of the world, but I ask you to protect them from the evil one. They do not belong to the world, just as I do not belong to the world. Sanctify them in the truth; your word is truth. As you have sent me into the world, so I have sent them into the world. And for their sakes I sanctify myself, so that they also may be sanctified in truth.

I ask not only on behalf of these, but also on behalf of those who will believe in me through their word, that they may all be one. As you, Father, are in me and I am in you, may they also be in us, so that the world may believe that you have sent me. The glory that you have given me I have given them, so that they may be one, as we are one, I in them and you in me, that they may become completely one, so that the world may know that you have sent me and have loved them even as you have loved me.

Father, I desire that those also, whom you have given me, may be with me where I am, to see my glory which you have given me because you loved me before the foundation of the world.

Righteous Father, the world does not know you, but I know you; and these know that you have sent me. I made your name known to them, and I will make it known, so that the love with which you have loved me may be in them, and I in them. (Jn 17)

THE OUR FATHER

Our Father in heaven, hallowed be your name. Your kingdom come. Your will be done, on earth as it is in heaven. Give us this day our daily bread. And forgive us our debts, as we also have forgiven our debtors. And do not bring us to the time of trial, but rescue us from the evil one. (Mt 6:9-13).

∞

Father, hallowed be your name. Your kingdom come. Give us each day our daily bread. And forgive us our sins, for we ourselves forgive everyone indebted to us. And do not bring us to the time of trial. (Lk 11:2-4).

∞

Some scholars have thought that the two versions represent teaching given on two different occasions. The more usual view is that they represent two traditions in the very early Church, both deriving from an Aramaic original. The three clauses given by Matthew but not by Luke contain ideas expressed by Jesus on other occasions and each of them is a development of a clause that is in both versions. The Church has always preferred Matthew's more ordered, more solemn text.

The poetic structure of the prayer comes through even in a vernacular translation. It is clearer in the New Testament Greek and clearer still when the Greek is translated into the original Aramaic. Like much of his teaching the prayer reveals the delightful fact that Jesus in his humanity was a poet.

Behind 'Father' is 'Abba', the intimate word with which Aramaic-speaking children addressed their father and which Jesus used in his own prayers. It denotes the new relationship with God that Jesus came to establish. Tertullian of the early Church called the Our Father *breviarium totius evangelii:* the gospel, the Good News, in brief.

The Christian community (or an individual member of that community) approaches a loving responsive Abba with certain petitions: requests related to the divine honour and requests touching directly on human needs.

In keeping with current Jewish reverence for the divine name the petitions of the first kind express the divine action in an indirect way. We are really praying: 'Abba, you ensure that you are truly recognised and valued, that you truly reign and rule, that you achieve your purpose in creation.' These petitions sum up the mindset and mission of Jesus himself. They give us an insight into the way he himself prayed.

Just as 'the kingdom' was central in Jesus' ministry, so is it central in his prayer. In union with him we pray that it may come in our own environment, in our own bit of history and geography but especially in that reality which he will usher in at his final coming.

In the 'bread' petition Matthew's Greek verb has a 'one-off' sense while Luke's has a continuous sense: 'keep on giving'. We ask for our daily sustenance and give thanks for what we receive and, desirably, share it with others. And the bread of life in the Eucharist may well come to mind.

The prayer links God's forgiveness of us and our forgiveness of one another in a kind of mutual mirroring, a kind of divine-human duet. It seems to be in parallel with Matthew 7:11 and Luke 11:13: 'If you know how to be good to your children (how to forgive), how much more will your Father be good to you (forgive you).' Some find it easy to forgive, others difficult. Some have an exaggerated and over-demanding idea of what forgiveness is and entails in their case: they need guidance. For all there is the grace to forgive (and to accept forgiveness) to ease them onto the river of peace.

The Greek *peirasmos* can mean 'temptation' in the ordinary sense but can also mean 'trial' or 'test'. Matthew's Greek word at the end can mean 'evil' or 'evil one'.

The 'Our Father' is a Christ-given reality which unites us in our here and now with our ancestors and successors in the faith. In it we celebrate our Abba and pray to be better citizens of Abba's kingdom as it develops towards its final glory and joy.

1. The Gethsemane prayer is a shattering statement of Jesus' humanity, of his depth-sharing in human experience. Matthew, Mark and Luke give his words of fear, struggle and loving obedience in substantially the same terms. Mark adds the precious 'Abba' which has meant so much to Christian faith and prayer.

Three of the 'words' from the Cross are explicit prayers. In two of them Jesus prays in texts taken from the prayer-treasury of his nation and culture: the psalms.

2. 'My God, my God...' This is the opening of the powerful psalm 21/22: a blend of anguish in the face of evil and of hope in God who does care and is ultimately victorious. Did Jesus say it all or have it all in mind? We do not know. The text as it stands is an unrelieved cry from the depths: no thanksgiving here, no self-offering, no intercession, no Abba-Father: rather a shout of pain: prayer at its extreme. It is a stark reminder of the enormity of his suffering, of the totality of his love.

3. 'Father, forgive them...' This is a supreme act of intercession, touching the very essence of his priestly mission. Luke's introductory verb is noteworthy: *elegen*: 'kept on saying'. The second 'word' given by Luke is a breathtaking answer to prayer. Here too we have *elegen*: 'He (the thief) kept on saying: Jesus, remember me...'

4. 'Into your hands...' is from psalm 30/31, enriched and made more poignant by 'Father (Abba)'. In the gospel of Luke this is the last word of the dying Lord. Appropriately this text is a constant refrain in the official night prayer of the Church.

THE PRAYERS OF JESUS

1. My Father, if it is possible, let this cup pass from
    me; yet not what I want but what you want.
    (Mt 26:39, Mk 14:36, Lk 22:42)

2. My God, my God, why have you forsaken me?
    (Mt 27:46, Mk 15:34)

3. Father, forgive them; for they know not what they
    are doing.' (Lk 23:34)

4. Father, into your hands I commend my spirit.
    (Lk 23:46)

1. Our Lady's response at the Annunciation is her surrender to God: the opening Greek word (traditionally translated 'behold') conveys 'here I am' and the Greek word for 'let it be' expresses humble desire.

2. The text of the *Magnificat* echoes (especially in its second half) the song of Anna in 1 Sam 2:1-10. It celebrates God's choice of Mary and emphasises God as the protector of the weak. The first few lines continue her Annunciation response and Elizabeth's salute of her. The prayer is in keeping with the humility and faith that we glimpse elsewhere in the New Testament. The reversals and contrasts in its second half and the emphasis on the divine mercy are consonant with the teaching of Jesus, especially in the gospel of Luke.

Mary surely expressed her joy at being a mother to Elizabeth but we do not have to believe that the *Magnificat* as it stands is her on-the-spot utterance. The evangelist, echoing his sources, is presenting her as the spokeswoman of gospel values, as the living example of those values, as the first disciple of Jesus, as the exemplar of all who serve God and are blessed by him. We can see the *Magnificat* as an expression of her engraced mature mind, as her 'mini-gospel'.

The western Church and Anglicans have the *Magnificat* in evening prayer, eastern liturgies in morning prayer. It is a central prayer of the Legion of Mary and has entered liberation theology. It has been much favoured by composers.

3. Her comment at Cana is an entrusting of the situation to her Son and in the evangelist's thinking an indication of her importance in the Christ-event.

THE PRAYERS OF OUR LADY

1. Here am I, the servant of the Lord; let it be with me according to your word. (Lk 1:38)

∽

2. My soul magnifies the Lord, and my spirit rejoices in God my Saviour, for he has looked with favour on the lowliness of his servant. Surely, from now on all generations will call me blessed; for the Mighty One has done great things for me, and holy is his name. His mercy is for those who fear him from generation to generation. He has shown strength with his arm; he has scattered the proud in the thoughts of their hearts. He has brought down the powerful from their thrones, and lifted up the lowly; he has filled the hungry with good things, and sent the rich away empty. He has helped his servant Israel, in remembrance of his mercy, according to the promise he made to our ancestors, to Abraham and to his descendants forever. (Lk 1:46-55)

∽

3. They have no wine. (Jn 2:3)

Luke surrounds the infant Jesus with three women and three men who served the God of Israel faithfully and looked forward to the coming of the promised Messiah: Mary, Elizabeth, Anna, Joseph, Zachary, Simeon. He associates four of them with texts of thanksgiving and praise.

1. Elizabeth's text praises God in the reality of the unborn Messiah and believing Mother.

2. Simeon's prayer is one of the most beautiful in the gospels: a very personal prayer about a duty done, a promise kept, a peace gained. Note how he emphasises that Jesus has come for the nations as well as for Israel (another Lukan theme). It was a happy thought to make Simeon's 'departure' the special refrain of the night prayer of the Church.

THE PRAYERS OF ELIZABETH AND SIMEON

1. Blessed are you among women, and blessed is the
fruit of your womb. And why has this happened to me,
that the mother of my Lord comes to me? For as soon
as I heard the sound of your greeting, the child in my
womb leaped for joy. And blessed is she who believed
that there would be a fulfilment of what was spoken to
her by the Lord. (Lk 1:42-45)

2. Master, now you are dismissing your servant in peace,
according to your word; for my eyes have seen your
salvation, which you have prepared in the presence of
all peoples, a light for revelation to the Gentiles and for
glory to your people Israel. (Lk 2:29-32)

In his *Benedictus* Zachary celebrates God's providence over Israel and God's choice of his son John as the fore-runner of the Messiah. He speaks of Christ as the revelation of the divine mercy (a major theme in Luke) and seems to compare him poetically to the rising sun. The concluding lines echo the beautiful blessing in Numbers 6:24-26. Appropriately the *Benedictus* is part of the morning ('rising sun') prayer of the Church.

THE PRAYER OF ZACHARY

Blessed be the Lord God of Israel, for he has looked favourably on his people and redeemed them. He has raised up a mighty Saviour for us in the house of his servant David, as he spoke through the mouth of his holy prophets from of old, that we would be saved from our enemies and from the hand of all who hate us. Thus he has shown the mercy promised to our ancestors, and has remembered his holy covenant, the oath that he swore to our ancestor Abraham, to grant us that we, being rescued from the hands of our enemies, might serve him without fear, in holiness and righteousness before him all our days. And you, child, will be called the prophet of the Most High; for you will go before the Lord to prepare his ways, to give knowledge of salvation to his people by the forgiveness of their sins. By the tender mercy of our God, the dawn from on high will break upon us, to give light to those who sit in darkness and in the shadow of death, to guide our feet into the way of peace. (Lk 1:68-79)

The relationship between Jesus and Peter is one of the most remarkable features of the gospels. From Peter's side it is often expressed in prayer.

1-5. At the lakeside his prayer is one of humility before the majesty of the Lord which has just been spectacularly manifested. In the storm-scene his cry for rescue signifies the lordship of Jesus and the Church's utter need of him. At Capernaum after the departure of many disciples he speaks for the Twelve in faith and longing, pathos and praise. At Caesarea Philippi he makes his great profession of faith (a renewal or development of his Capernaum prayer) and receives the great promise of stewardship of the Church. At the lakeside again, this time at dawn of day in the presence of the risen Christ, he atones for the three denials on the night of the Passion with three avowals of love.

Countless Christians have made these prayers of Peter their own.

THE PRAYERS OF PETER

1. Go away from me, Lord, for I am a sinful man! (Lk 5:8)

2. Lord, save me! (Mt 14:30)

3. Lord, to whom can we go? You have the words of
    eternal life. We have come to believe and know that
    you are the Holy One of God. (Jn 6:68-69)

4. You are the Messiah, the Son of the living God.
    (Mt 16:16)

5. You know that I love you …
    You know that I love you …
    Lord, you know everything;
    you know that I love you.(Jn 21:15-17)

1. Here Thomas gives us one of the greatest of gospel moments, representing all believers before the crucified and risen One.

2. In their 'Stay with us', saying more than they know, Cleophas and his companion represent countless Christians asking that the same One may be with them in their journey of faith.

3. 'The disciple whom Jesus loved' (traditionally identified with John) in his wonder and welcome surely stands for all who find the presence of Jesus the greatest gift and the best reason for joy.

4. Martha, mourning for her dead brother, sees Jesus as intercessor and guarantor of life and rivals Peter in her profession of faith.

5. Mary Magdalene, clinging to the risen Lord, salutes him with one word. 'Rabbouni' is a solemn form of the Aramaic word for 'Teacher'. It was often used as a title for God. Here it may well be Mary's equivalent of Thomas' 'My Lord and my God', making it one of the greatest of gospel prayers.

THE PRAYERS OF THE DISCIPLES

1. My Lord and my God! (Jn 20:28)

☙

2. Stay with us, because it is almost evening and the day is now nearly over. (Lk 24:29)

☙

3. It is the Lord! (Jn 21:7)

☙

4. Lord, I believe that you are the Messiah, the Son of God, the one coming into the world. (Jn 11:27)

☙

5. Rabbouni! (Jn 20:16).

Nearly all of those came to Jesus for help were the 'little ones' who had a special place in his heart. At times they asked silently by presence and gesture. But nearly always there would have been words; and some of these have been immortalised in the gospels, adding significantly to their realism and human interest. Often asking for others, these gospel suppliants are among the pioneers of a vast volume of Jesus-focused prayer (much of it intercession) down the centuries.

1-3. Matthew, Mark and Luke show us the sick man ('full of leprosy', says Luke the physician) on his knees and Jesus' stretched-out and touching hand. John tells us in detail of the official and his son. The sick child is at Capernaum on the lakeshore. Jesus is at Cana on higher ground; so the official asks him to 'come down'. Matthew and Mark highlight the remarkable Syro-Phoenician mother fighting for her afflicted daughter and winning her verbal duel with Jesus.

4-6. Of the three accounts of the frantic father and his epileptic son, Mark's is the most graphic and is specially notable for a profound and precious conversation piece between Jesus and the father. Luke has his exclusive collective cure scene with its emphasis on gratitude for favours received. The episode of the persistent blind man of Jericho (Mark identifies him as 'the son of Timaeus) is part of the finale of Jesus' ministry before the onset of his Passion. The use of a royal title ('Son of David') enhances the prayer and points to the messianic excitement focused on the Lord.

THE PRAYERS OF THE PEOPLE

1. Lord, if you choose, you can make me clean.
   (Mt 8:2; Mk 1:40; Lk 5:12)

2. Sir, come down before my little boy dies. (Jn 4:49)

3. Have mercy on me, Lord, Son of David; my
   daughter is tormented by a demon ... Lord, help me.
   (Mt 15:22, 25)

4. If you are able to do anything, have pity on us and
   help us ... I believe, help my unbelief. (Mk 9:22-24)

5. Jesus, Master, have mercy on us! (Lk 17:13)

6. Jesus, Son of David, have mercy on me ...
   Son of David, have mercy on me ...
   My teacher, let me see again.
   (Mk 10:47, 48, 51)

1. The 'Sovereign Lord' prayer represents the mind of the very early Christian community in a time of stress. It combines Jewish and Christian elements. There is one God, creator of all, who has spoken in prophecy and promised the Messiah. Jesus is the servant-Messiah and his disciples continue his mission and witness to him in word and healing; and like him they experience opposition.

2. With Stephen the mission becomes martyrdom. He proclaims the risen Christ and in his prayers he echoes the prayers of Jesus on the Cross. The message is that the dying Christian is to share the mind and heart of the dying Christ.

3. Saul-Paul's first prayer that we have record of is a question. He grasps that the Damascus Road experience is 'from heaven': his 'Lord' is a confused reference to the God of Abraham, Isaac and Jacob. The answer shatteringly identifies his 'Lord' with Jesus and transforms his life.

PRAYERS IN THE ACTS OF THE APOSTLES

1. Sovereign Lord, who made the heaven and the earth, the sea, and everything in them, it is you who said by the Holy Spirit through our ancestor David, your servant: 'Why did the Gentiles rage, and the peoples imagine vain things?

And now, Lord, look at their threats, and grant to your servants to speak your word with all boldness, while you stretch out your hand to heal, and signs and wonders are performed through the name of your holy servant Jesus. (4:24-25, 29-30)

∞

2. I see the heavens opened and the Son of Man standing at the right hand of God! … Lord Jesus, receive my spirit … Lord do not hold this sin against them.' (7:56, 59-60)

∞

3. Who are you, Lord? (9:5)

The Epistles are punctuated with prayers and hymns, many of them outbursts of praise. Three of the five texts selected here occur as canticles in the official prayer of the Church.

1. In chapter 1-11 of Romans Paul is at his most theological, delving into such things as sin, grace, faith, glory, 'Abba' life in Christ and the Spirit, God's mercy for both Jews and Gentiles. After all that, he utters his 'depth' prayer, incorporating a few lines from Isaiah. There is a similar prayer at the end of the epistle with a similar stress on wisdom.

2. This prayer is Paul's great proclamation of the 'cosmic Christ'. The Christians of Colossae were exposed to beliefs and observances that threatened their new-found Christian faith. In words that recall the opening lines of the gospel of John, Paul insists on the centrality and uniqueness of Christ. He also asserts the datable reality of his death and resurrection. In all this Christ is in sharp contrast to 'the elemental spirits' of certain 'philosophers'. Colossians is a very Christocentric epistle and very relevant today.

PRAYERS IN THE EPISTLES

1. O the depth of the riches and wisdom and knowledge of God! How unsearchable are his judgments and how inscrutable his ways!

For who has known the mind of the Lord? Or who has been his counsellor? Or who has given a gift to him, to receive a gift in return?

For from him and through him and to him are all things. To him be the glory forever. Amen.
(Rom 11:33-36)

2. He is the image of the invisible God, the firstborn of all creation; for in him all things in heaven and on earth were created, things visible and invisible, whether thrones or dominions or rulers or powers – all things have been created through him and for him. He himself is before all things, and in him all things hold together. He is the head of the body, the church; he is the beginning, the firstborn from the dead, so that he might come to have first place in everything. For in him all the fullness of God was pleased to dwell, and through him God was pleased to reconcile to himself all things, whether on earth or in heaven, by making peace through the blood of his cross. (Col 1:15-20)

1. Ephesians is a companion epistle to Colossians. It is thought to have been a general letter to various communities rather than to one. The panoramic opening prayer is a proclamation of God's mind/purpose/plan in Christ. 'The Father' is sovereign, free, wise, forgiving, life-sharing. The prayer beautifully calls Christ 'the Beloved' (in keeping with the episodes of his baptism and transfiguration) and ends with a glimpse of the 'cosmic Christ'. It is richly 'spelled out' in the epistle. (A very doctrinal letter is Ephesians). There is a somewhat similar prayer in 1 Peter 1:3-5.

2. This 'flesh to glory' prayer echoes Paul's teaching on Christ in Colossians. It looks or sounds very like a liturgical hymn or acclamation or creed. If it is, it is a striking testimony to the Christ-centred faith of the very early Church. It, or a paraphrase of it, would make a splendid acclamation of welcome to the Lord in the Mass.

3. The epistle to the Hebrews emphasises the humanity and priesthood of Jesus. Here it makes part of psalm 39/40 into a prayer of self-offering by Jesus at his coming into the world. But consonantly with his purpose the writer struck out part of a verse of the psalm and substituted 'a body you have prepared for me'. Another text (5:7) refers to Jesus' prayer in Gethsemane.

PRAYERS IN THE EPISTLES

1. Blessed be the God and Father of our Lord Jesus Christ, who has blessed us in Christ with every spiritual blessing in the heavenly places, just as he chose us in Christ before the foundation of the world to be holy and blameless before him in love. He destined us for adoption as his children through Jesus Christ, according to the good pleasure of his will, to the praise of his glorious grace that he freely bestowed on us in the Beloved. In him we have redemption through his blood, the forgiveness of our trespasses, according to the riches of his grace that he lavished on us. With all wisdom and insight he has made known to us the mystery of his will, according to his good pleasure that he set forth in Christ, as a plan for the fullness of time, to gather up all things in him, things in heaven and things on earth… (Eph 1:3-10)

2. He was revealed in flesh, vindicated in spirit, seen by angels, proclaimed among Gentiles, believed in throughout the world, taken up in glory. (1 Tim 3:16)

3. Sacrifices and offerings you have not desired, but a body you have prepared for me; in burnt offerings and sin offerings you have taken no pleasure. Then I said, 'See, God, I have come to do your will, O God' (in the scroll of the book it is written of me.) (Heb 10:5-7)

Written at a time of persecution, with a wealth of image and symbol Revelation presents the struggle between good and evil and the final victory of God and his people. It abounds in praise-passages, most of which occur as canticles in the Divine Office. The first and last of them are given here.

1-2. The first recalls the Thrice-Holy of Isaiah's experience of the God of majesty (Is 6:1-3). The last and greatest resounds with 'Alleluia', the Hebrew acclamation which Christians appropriated for the Christ-event, and announces the definitive union of Christ and his people.

3. Towards the end of Revelation the music slows down, the melody is broad and flowing, the refrain is 'Come': 'I am coming soon … The Spirit and the bride say, "Come." And let everyone who hears say, "Come." And let everyone who is thirsty come … The one who testifies to these things says, "Surely I am coming soon." Amen. Come, Lord Jesus!'

On this note of longing and hope the New Testament ends.

PRAYERS IN THE BOOK OF REVELATION

1. Holy, holy, holy,
the Lord God the Almighty,
who was and is and is to come. (Rev 4:8)

∞

2. Hallelujah! Salvation and glory and power to our
God, for his judgements are true and just ... Amen.
Hallelujah! ... Praise our God all you his servants, and
all who fear him, small and great ... Hallelujah! For the
Lord our God the Almighty reigns. Let us rejoice and
exult and give him the glory, for the marriage of the
Lamb has come, and his bride has made herself ready..
(Rev 19:1-7)

∞

3. Come, Lord Jesus! (Rev 22:20)

1. 'We are Easter people', said Saint Augustine 'and Alleluia is our song'. 'Alleluia' is a Hebrew word: 'Hallelu: praise (verb, imperative mood) and 'Ya' (short for Yahweh: Lord). Christians brought this temple and synagogue word into their own prayers, applying it to the Christ-event especially the resurrection. Happily untranslated, it mellifluously rolls off the tongue and calls out to be sung – as indeed it has in numberless settings. In the 'Alleluia' we are part of a tri-millennial chorus.

The new Testament is really a record of praise and thanksgiving for the Christ-event. Praise-texts include the *Magnificat* and *Benedictus* and 'Glory to God in high heaven' in the gospel of Luke, the beginning of Ephesians, the 'Christ-hymn' in Colossians, the finale of Romans and the Alleluia sequence in Revelation.

2. Scholars connect the 'Glory be to the Father' with the fourth-century Arian crisis. Defenders of the divinity of Christ against the Arians promoted a formula of 'Person-equality' taken from the finale of Matthew's gospel. The Latin-using west added *sicut erat in principio* (as it was in the beginning) to re-emphasise the divinity of the Son and doubtless that of the Holy Spirit whose divinity had also been denied.

3. Another Catholic response to the Arians was, it seems certain, the *Te Deum*. Its first and second parts (given here) extol the Trinity and Christ in his incarnation and echo the anti-Arian creed we proclaim at Mass. It may have been written by Nicetas, bishop of Ramesiana in the present Serbia. Composers have loved it. We sing it as 'Holy God'.

2. PRAISE THE LORD

1. Alleluia!

࿊

2. Glory be to the Father and to the Son and to the Holy Spirit. As it was in the beginning, is now and every shall be, world without end. Amen.

࿊

3. ** We praise you, our God. We acknowledge you to be the Lord. All the earth worships you, eternal Father. All the angels, all the powers of heaven, the cherubim and seraphim unceasingly proclaim: Holy, Holy, Holy, Lord God of armies. Heaven and earth are filled with your greatness and glory. The glorious company of apostles, all the prophets deserving of praise, the shining ranks of martyrs, the holy Church throughout the world – all praise you: Father of immeasurable greatness, your true and only Son worthy of veneration and the Holy Spirit the faithful friend.

You, Christ, are the king of glory and the eternal Son of the Father. About to undertake the freeing of the human family, you did not shrink from the Virgin's womb. You overcame the sting of death and opened the kingdom of heaven to those who believe. You are seated at the right hand of God in the glory of the Father. We believe that you will come as judge. And so we beseech you to help your servants whom you have redeemed by your precious blood. Grant that we may be numbered among your saints in eternal glory.

1. The 'Gloria' is a development of the Christmas text in the gospel of Luke. Its earliest known Latin text (shorter than ours) is in the seventh-century antiphonary of the monastery of Bangor near the present Belfast. Said to have been first confined to Christmas, it was eventually used on all feast-days. With the number of feast-days reduced since Vatican II this dynamic prayer now occurs more rarely.

2. The prayers at the offering of the bread and wine, introduced into the Mass after Vatican II are taken almost verbatim from the 'Mishnah (Repetition)', the book of rabbinic instruction. They are an ecumenical reminder of the Jewish source of much of our worship.

3. As is the *Tersanctus:* this recalls Isaiah's temple experience (Is 6). There is evidence that Christians in Rome had this prayer shortly after the time of Christ but it is not certain that it was then in the Mass. It was certainly in the Roman Mass by the sixth century and in at least a few eastern liturgies long before that. We need not confine it to the Mass. With its 'earth filled with your glory' it is an 'environment' prayer.

4-5. In keeping with early Church practice (and doubtless in friendship towards Protestant and Orthodox Christians) the post-Vatican II reform inserted an ancient praise-formula after the Our Father. But the climactic praise-statement in the Mass is that at the end of the Eucharistic Prayer. This prayer is very ancient and is consonant with a third-century Roman text. And the people's Amen is their 'signature' to the great Deed just done, to the whole Christ-event.

1. Glory to God in high heaven and peace to all of loving heart. We praise you, bless you, glorify you, thank you because of your great glory: Lord God, heavenly King, God the Almighty Father.

Lord Jesus Christ, only-begotten Son, Lord God, Lamb of God, Son of the Father: you take away the sins of the world, have mercy on us; you take away the sins of the world, receive our prayer; you are seated at the right hand of the Father, have mercy on us: for you alone are the Holy One, you alone are the Lord, you alone are the Most High: Jesus Christ with the Holy Spirit in the glory of God the Father. Amen.

2. Blessed are you, Lord, God of all creation. Of your goodness we have received this bread/this wine which we offer you: fruit of the earth/fruit of the vine and work of human hands: it will become for us the bread of life/spiritual drink. Blessed be God forever.

3. Holy, Holy, Holy, Lord God of armies!
Heaven and earth are filled with your glory!

4. Yours is the kingdom and the power and the glory forever!

5. Through him and with him and in him, to you God the Almighty Father, in the unity of the Holy Spirit, is all honour and glory forevermore. Amen.

The Mass in the Roman rite is very much *ad Patrem,* to the Father. But here and there in its fixed texts it has prayers addressed to Christ. *Kyrie eleison* (Lord, have mercy) came into the Roman Mass in the early fifth century. Pope Gregory the Great (590-604) twinned it with *Christe eleison.* For many centuries the six *Kyrie* and three *Christe* invocations formed a Greek enclave in a Mass otherwise Latin except for *Hosanna* and *Sabaoth* just after the Preface. The prayer is still with us but reduced from nine invocations to three and nearly always in the vernacular.

2-3. The gospel represents Christ, so it is fitting that he should be acclaimed immediately before and after it is read. These formulas have been in the Roman Mass for more than a millennium.

4. The 'Holy, Holy, Holy' came into the Roman Mass at an early date and was soon joined by the Palm Sunday acclamation of Jesus as given in Matthew 21:9 and Mark 11:9-10. The Aramaic *Hosanna* (Hebrew *Hosiahna*) means 'Save, we pray' but it was also used as something like our 'Hurrah'.

5. The liturgical reform after Vatican II introduced acclamations after the words of institution in the Eucharistic Prayer. Irish-speaking congregations anticipated the Council by centuries. Three of these moving and intimate salutes of our ancestors in the faith are given here. Perhaps they have something to teach us.

3. FOCUS ON JESUS

1. Lord, have mercy.
   Christ, have mercy.
   Lord, have mercy

   ∽

2. Glory to you, Lord

   ∽

3. Praise to you, Lord Jesus Christ

   ∽

4. Hosanna in the highest
   Blessed is he who comes in the name of the Lord
   Hosanna in the highest

   ∽

5. A hundred thousand welcomes, Lord
   Welcome to you, Saviour Jesus Christ
   A hundred thousand welcomes to you, King of Sunday

1. The beautiful prayer for peace is partly derived from the discourse after the Last Supper. (Jn 14:27)

2. In the 'Lamb of God' prayer we share in John the Baptist's recognition of Jesus as given in John 1:29. Eastern Christians thought of Jesus in the Eucharist as the sacrificed and glorified Lamb of the Book of Revelation and clergy fleeing before Islam brought the idea to Rome. This prayer which acclaims the Lord as Saviour of the world came into the Roman Mass in the seventh century, probably introduced by Pope Sergius 1 who was himself from Syria. At first it accompanied the breaking of the species of bread. When 'hosts' came into use the sequence was greatly shortened, became attached to the sign of peace and to Communion, and was rounded off by 'grant us peace'.

3. Before Communion the priest says one of two prayers. The 'Son of the living God' prayer amounts to a mini-creed and asks for Christian basics. These two prayers and the prayer for peace began to appear in the Roman Mass about a millennium ago.

4. The military rank most mentioned in the New Testament is that of centurion: the equivalent, more or less, of the modern non-commissioned officer. The centurion of Capernaum has been immortalised in the Mass for centuries in both eastern and western liturgies. Let us pray at this point for others as well as for ourselves; after all, the good man whose words we use was asking for someone else: 'I am not worthy that you should enter under my roof. Only say the word and my servant will be healed.' (Mt 8, Lk 7)

1. Lord Jesus Christ, you said to your apostles:
   peace I leave you, my peace I give you.
   Do not look on our sins but on the faith of your
   Church and graciously grant it peace and unity
   according to your will.

   ∞

2. Lamb of God, you take away the sins of the world
   have mercy on us… have mercy on us… grant us peace.

   ∞

3. Lord Jesus Christ, Son of the living God
   by the will of the Father and the co-working of the
   Holy Spirit,
   through your death you have given life to the world.
   By your most holy Body and Blood free me from all
   my sins and from every evil,
   make me always hold fast to your commandments,
   and never let me be parted from you.

   ∞

4. Lord, I am not worthy that you should enter under
   my roof, but only say the word and I shall be healed.

1. This prayer of longing and hope is almost the last sentence of the New Testament (Rev 22:20). 'Come, Lord' translates the Aramaic *Maranatha* – which can also but less probably mean 'the Lord is coming' or 'the Lord has come'. Saint Paul has *Maranatha* at the end of his first letter to the Greek-speaking Christians of Corinth, which indicates that it was already in Christian worship. It seems certain that New Testament Christians applied the word both to Christ's coming in the Eucharist and to his final coming in glory – as we can too.

2. The 'Jesus Prayer' is the heart of a method of meditation practised mostly in the Orthodox Church. The prayer (which has various forms) is repeated in faith, hope and love and combined with a concentration on breathing, heart-beat and muscle-flexing. The aim is to steep oneself in the presence of God and to be united with God in deep peace.

This form of prayer can be traced back at least to the fifth century. Something like it can be found in the teaching of Saints Bernard, Bernardine and Ignatius Loyola. The 'father' of its present popularity is the monastic founder and writer Paissy Velitchkovsky (1722-1794).

3. Aurelius Prudentius Clemens (b. 348) was the foremost Latin poet in the Church in its first century of freedom of worship in the Roman State. Seven of his poems, including this morning hymn, were accepted into the Divine Office.

1. Come, Lord Jesus1

    ∽

2. Lord Jesus Christ, Son of God, have mercy on me

    ∽

3.**

    Night and the dark and clouds
    tumultuous, in rout
    Depart! – the sky is whitening, Christ is near
    Sun-arrows pierce the mist
    and colour's coming out
    and look! – the morning star is shining clear.

    So will our troubled mind
    our wilful heart and sense
    find healing when the Lord is seen to reign
    Christ, our redeeming Friend
    we mourn our sin, offence
    and knowing you, we rise in hope again

    See us and all we are
    all we have ever done
    dear radiant light of healing purity
    Glory to you, dear Christ
    with Father and Spirit one
    all praise to you, eternal Trinity. Amen

In 669 the emperor Justin sent a reputed relic of the
True Cross to the Frankish queen Radegunda. Her court
poet, Venantius Fortunatus, wrote the *Vexilla Regis* (The
Banners of the King) for the occasion. He may also have
composed its beautiful plainsong melody. In her famous
The Wandering Scholars, Helen Waddell called it the
greatest processional of the Middle Ages. Crusaders to
the Holy Land made it their special hymn. Only part of
the *Vexilla* is given here.

**

The banners of the King advance
the Cross is shining mystery
and Life in Person suffers death
by death gives life, makes free

A wounded King, the wood his throne
a final thrust: the lance goes in
and blood and water from his Heart
to cleanse our hearts from sin

A tree so beautiful: adorned
with royal purple, precious blood
a tree that touches sacred limbs
a tree that's chosen wood

Dear blessed tree, your branches held
the Ransom for the world's distress
you weighed the Ransom, foiled the foe
of fruits of wickedness

Fortunatus also wrote the *Pange Lingua Gloriosi Lauream Certaminis* (Proclaim the Triumph…) in honour of the relic. In this celebration of Christ the Victor he appropriately wrote in a 'military' metre: trochaic tetrameter, a rhythm used for marching songs in the Roman army. For these two meditative masterpieces he is deservedly called 'the poet of the Holy Cross'. They are in the liturgy of Holy Week. That great treasure of the early English Church, 'The Dream of the Rood', is in the same tradition. Only part of the *Pange* is given here.

**

Cross so faithful! Tree of trees, the noblest tree that ever
    stood

never did a forest bear such glorious flower and leaf and
    bud

Sweet the wood and nails that hold the sweetest weight
    of flesh and blood

Bend your branches, towering tree, and welcome this
    most special guest

Make your members soft and yielding, cradle him upon
    your breast

He's your Maker, treat him gently, set the limbs of Love
    at rest

Worthy wood and chosen timber, ransom-bearer, tool of
    grace

pilot sent to bring to port the wandering sin-wrecked
    human race

blood-anointed, consecrated, set apart in Love's
    embrace

1. The *Sancti Venite* (Come, Holy Ones) is the best-known eucharistic hymn of the early Irish Church. It is found in the *Antiphonary of Bangor* (now in the Ambrosian Library, Milan), compiled in the great monastery on the shore of Belfast Lough at the end of the seventh century. The doctrine of the sacrament is stated clearly, the invitation to partake is given solemnly. There is an impression of discipline: a procession, rather than a pressing-forward, to the altar.

2. The Breastplate of St Patrick is partly an invocation of the Blessed Trinity and partly an invocation of Christ. This celebrated morning prayer of the early Irish Church is a wonderful expression of that sense of Christ's intimate presence, so characteristic of Irish spirituality.

1.** Come all in him, share in his Body,
    Come, and receive, drink his redeeming Blood.
    Eucharist-saved, nourished in sacrament
    come let us sing our praise to God.

    Body and Blood: sacrament setting free
    we have been saved, rescued from Satan's pit
    given for all, Saviour in sacrifice
    he is the priest and he is gift.

    Come nearer still, pure and with faith in him
    let all receive gifts that will save and guard
    First and the last, Alpha and Omega
    One who will come, the judge, the Lord.

        ○○

2. Christ with me
    Christ before me
    Christ behind me
    Christ within me
    Christ beneath me
    Christ above me
    Christ at my right hand
    Christ at my left hand
    Christ where I shall lie
    Christ where I shall sit
    Christ where I shall stand
    Christ in the heart of everyone who thinks of me
    Christ in the mouth of everyone who speaks to me
    Christ in every eye that looks on me
    Christ in every ear that listens to me.

1. Pilgrims to the Holy Land, and also the more devout of the crusaders of the twelfth and thirteenth centuries, on returning home set up representations of pilgrim places. These became known as 'stations' (stopping-places) and were finally limited to the Way of the Cross itself and standardised in subject-matter and number. The Franciscans, who were the custodians of the Holy Places, made the 'stations' a special apostolate. The prayer given here of Saint Francis, who was of course utterly devoted to Jesus in his Passion, became (and still is) a standard part of 'doing the stations'.

2. One of the most attractive prayers to the Lord in the Eucharist is the thirteenth-century *Adoro Te Devote*. It may have been written by Saint Thomas Aquinas. It blends scripture and theology. The tone is tender and personalised. And it has been blessed with a delightful and simple plainsong setting. The first and last stanzas are given here.

3. The antiphon *O Sacrum Convivium* (O Sacred Banquet), from the Office of Corpus Christi, says much in a few words. With its scriptural background of the Last Supper, and of at least the second half of the bread of life discourse in John 6, it is an admirable summary of eucharistic doctrine. It has much in common with the reading from Saint Thomas Aquinas in the same Office.

1. We adore you, O Christ, and we bless you because
    by your holy Cross you have redeemed the world

    ∞

2.** Deeply I adore you, veiled divinity
underneath the signs I see you are truly here
and to you I surrender, Love so strong, so near
contemplating you, my Love, leads to ecstasy

Now I turn to you in faith: you are veiled from me
hidden Jesus, hear my prayer, grant this longed-for grace
bring me out of the shadowlands, let me see your face
in your glory let me find joy eternally. Amen.

    ∞

3.** Holy Banquet, heaven-sent,
Christ himself our nourishment,
proclaiming of his Passion and his death on Calvary.
Gift to fill the heart with grace
till we see him face to face,
promise of eternal life, of future glory.

The *Pange lingua gloriosi Corporis mysterium,* given here in translation, is one of the greatest hymns ever written in honour of the Blessed Sacrament. It is in the Office of Corpus Christi and in the liturgy of Holy Thursday. Along with the other hymns of Corpus Christi (*Verbum Supernum:* Word from Heaven and *Sacris Solemniis:* Sacred Solemnities) it is a brilliant blend of doctrine, devotion and verse-technique and is traditionally ascribed to Saint Thomas Aquinas (d. 1274); but his authorship is strongly disputed. He may have been the editor of the Office rather than its author. The last two stanzas of the *Pange* and the *Verbum* became the standard hymns for Benediction of the Blessed Sacrament as *Tantum ergo* and *O Salutaris* respectively.

Like the other *Pange,* Fortunatus' masterpiece 'Song of Victory', it is written in trochaic tetrameter, a rhythm used in Roman army marching songs: it helps the 'proclamation' element in the message. This metre has been kept in translations of both hymns in this book.

**

Make a song to celebrate this eucharistic mystery
glorious Body, precious Blood, the ransom paid to set
    us free
Mary's son, the Lord of nations, Heart of God's own
    liturgy

Given to us and born for us of Mary ever-virginal
giving us the gospel word to know the Father, hear his call
ending life as priest and gift in one momentous festival

Supper-room and friends together; paschal moon; his
    final night
Exodus: the great tradition, legal forms and ancient rite
then he gives himself as food: an act of love, an act of might

Word-made-flesh makes bread his flesh: with just a
    word the deed is done
then the cup: the wine becomes the precious Blood of
    Mary's Son
senses fail and faith alone assures the mind that Christ
    has come

Let us therefore venerate this greatest of the sacraments
patterns of the past foretold this crowning act of provid-
    ence
let our faith enrich our mind, discover all that's veiled to
sense

To the Father, to the Son incarnate in this mystery
praise and glory, power, thanksgiving, as it was, is now,
    shall be
to their Love, the Holy Spirit, equal praise eternally.
Amen.

1. If you are ever in Seville, visit the Alcazar and look at the doorway of the Hall of Charles v. There you will see inscribed in Latin most of the *Anima Christi*: 'Soul of Christ…'. The inscription is dated 1364. Twenty years earlier a German mystic, Margaret Ebner, referred to the prayer in her spiritual journal: 'And so I prayed … *Anima Christi, sanctifica me,* and I implored that I might be strengthened by his suffering …'

We do not know who composed this poignant prayer. It has been credited to Pope John XXII (1316-1334). It was a great favourite of Saint Ignatius Loyola and he recommended it in his *Spiritual Exercises*. It was also highly esteemed by John Henry Newman who called it 'my creed'. We sing it as 'Soul of my Saviour'.

2-3. Devotion to the Lord in his Passion is strong in the Gaelic-speaking Catholic tradition. Two expressions of that devotion are given here, one from Scotland, one from Ireland.

1. Soul of Christ, sanctify me,
   Body of Christ, save me,
   Blood of Christ, enrapture me,
   Water from the side of Christ, wash me,
   Passion of Christ, strengthen me.
   O good Jesus, hear me,
   within your wounds hide me,
   from the malicious enemy defend me,
   never let me be parted from you,
   at the hour of my death call me and bid me come to you,
   that with your saints I may praise you for ever more.
   Amen.

   ☙

2. ** Jesus! Begotten Son, the Lamb of God
   redeeming me you gave your life's wine-blood
   My Christ, my Christ, encircling power
   by day, by night, by hour

   ☙

3. ** Lord, a drop from the holy Cross
   to penetrate me deep within
   to lift the grief, to show the truth
   to free me from all stain and sin

Cor Arca Legem Continens (Heart of Grace) is from the office of the Solemnity of the Sacred Heart of Jesus. Originally in five stanzas, it is usually dated to the eighteenth century and can be said to pertain to the development of devotion to the Heart of Christ initiated by Saints Margaret Mary and Claude la Colombiere. It is strongly scriptural. In stanzas three, four and five the unknown author echoes the mystical theology of the thirteenth-century Franciscan Saint Bonaventure.

**

You are the ark that holds the law
not of the former slavery:
law of forgiveness, mercy, grace
that sets us free

Heart that's the house of covenant
holy ground here – let none deface
temple of temples heaven-sent
the veil of grace

Heart that was opened: water, blood
symbols of life, of death to sin
wounds of the Word to show the way
to Love within

Heart that's the sign of total gift
given in blood and Eucharist
Supper and Cross and ever since
Christ is the priest

Lover and Love! Who, loved like this,
would not love too and keep a tryst
lasting forever heart-to-heart
and cling to Christ?

Praise to the Father and Spirit-Friend
praise to the Son, the Heart of Grace
bring us from shadows into light
to see your face. Amen

If it is true, as Saint Augustine said, that 'singing is for lovers', we would expect singing to be associated with the Spirit who in the Trinity is the uncreated mutual Love of the Father and the Son.

At least two sung masterpieces are dedicated to the Spirit: the *Veni, Creator Spiritus* and the *Veni, Sancte Spiritus*. The oldest known manuscript of the former is of the tenth century and its earliest recorded use is at the Council of Rheims in 1049. It was made part of the liturgy of ordination and of the office of Pentecost.

We do not know who wrote this profound prayer which has echoed in the ordination-day memories of countless priests. A work surely of the cultural movement that developed in western Europe in the eighth and ninth centuries, it has been attributed to Charlemagne himself, who initiated and promoted that movement, and to the abbot and archbishop, Rabanus Maurus, one of its leading lights.

We nearly always have it in Caswell's translation 'Come, O Creator Spirit blest' sung to Webbe's melody – and very impressive it can be. But nothing can really replace the Latin text and buoyant lilting plain-chant.

4. CELEBRATING THE HOLY SPIRIT

**

Come, O Creator Spirit, come
welcome to you, dear Friend, today
fill all the hearts that you have made
Come, Spirit, stay

Gift that is God and Friend at hand
listening, understanding, freeing
fountain alive and fire and love
balm of our being

Finger of God, the Promised One
rich in your gifts, engracing Lord
Spirit that moves the heart and mind
to speak the word

Come, Spirit, give our senses light
come, Spirit, love us through and through
come, Spirit, heal our body's ills
refresh, renew

Rescue us from the evil one
give us a peace that's swift and strong
You be our guide: we'll do your will
keep clear of wrong

Through you, dear Spirit, may we know
the Father of all, the Word, the Son
strengthen our faith in you, dear Friend
come, Spirit, come

1-2. Also in the office of Pentecost are 'Come... fill the hearts and 'Send forth your Spirit'. They are often combined into one prayer. The 'Send forth' is taken from one of the greatest of the psalms, psalm 103/104, which proclaims the creative and conserving power of God. It is a prayer to remind us of our God-given natural environment and of the engraced integration of creation into the Christ-event (see Romans 8:19-23).

3. In the official prayer of the Church the 'third hour' (mid-morning) office is dedicated to the Holy Spirit in memory of Pentecost (see Acts of the Apostles 2:15). One of the hymns of that office is given here: we ask the Spirit to dwell in us and draw us to the Father and the Son.

1. Come, Holy Spirit, fill the hearts of your faithful
   and enkindle in them the fire of your love.

2. Send forth your Spirit, Lord, and they shall be created.
   And you shall renew the face of the earth.

3.** Holy Spirit, you are Lord
   one with Father, one with Word
   come now-now, do not delay
   fill our very being today

   Bless our mind and sense and tongue
   make us singers of your song
   you are Love and love's your art
   bind us, Spirit, heart to heart

   Through you, Spirit, may we come
   to know the Father, know the Son
   know you too, dear Spirit-Friend
   share a joy that has no end. Amen.

The nouns and verbs of the prayers celebrating the Holy Spirit try to convey a Reality that is divinely dynamic, sovereignly free, intimately near: light, fire, fountain, truth, love, gift, anointing, Paraclete (someone called alongside); come, dwell, fill, enlighten, enkindle, purify, strengthen, renew.

The Spirit gets great attention in the liturgy, being invoked in the sacramental formulas of baptism, confirmation, holy orders, penance and the sacrament of the sick; and since Vatican II being explicitly invoked at the heart of the Mass just before the Last Supper words of institution.

The special day of celebration of the Holy Spirit is of course Pentecost. A highlight of the festival Mass is the *Veni, Sancte Spiritus,* the sequence sung or said before the gospel. A dynamic prayer this, with its swift transitions and rhythm somehow suggesting the Pentecost wind. Its images are a wonderful evocation of what the Spirit is and means in our life of union with God. The Latin text and plainsong melody form an exquisite artistic unity. It has been well-named 'the Golden Sequence'. A very slightly condensed version is given here.

It dates from the late twelfth century. It has been credited to Lothar of Segni, Pope Innocent III (1198-1216); but scholars are strongly inclined to give the honour to Stephen Langton, student and teacher at the University of Paris and later Archbishop of Canterbury and one of the authors of Magna Carta.

**

Come, Holy Spirit, come
come, pour from heaven's fount
your radiance, your light

Come, Father of the poor
come, giver of all gifts
come, light that fills our heart

The One who strengthens most
our being's gentle guest
the Friend refreshing friends

Our rest in all distress
control in passion's storm
and solace in our grief

Come, most blessed light
fill the depths, the hearts
of all you call your own

Without your power and will
our nature is bereft
of all that's innocent

We are sick – come, heal
we are soiled– come, cleanse
we are cold – come, warm

Give to all your friends
to all who hope in you
the sacred seven gifts

Fulfil all good they've done
make death the way to life
and give eternal joy. Amen.

1. The Holy Spirit is much honoured among eastern Christians. 'Heavenly King', presented here in verse, is a traditional eastern morning and evening prayer. It is full of doctrine and completely consonant with its western counterparts.

3. One such counterpart is 'Holy Spirit heaven-sent' from the Gaelic-speaking Catholic tradition in Scotland. It emphasises the Spirit as the bond of love and echoes the Our Father.

1.** Spirit, heaven's King, the Strengthener
   Truth and Life, the Presence everywhere
   the Giver given
   Spirit, come! – engrace us through and through
   Spirit, dwell in us, refresh, renew
   keep safe for heaven.

2.** The Holy Spirit, heaven-sent, poured, given
   to bind my prayers to you
   the King of all there is
   to help me live anew
   be in your love, your family
   your will, your care, reality
   to live on earth like this
   to choose what saints and angels choose in heaven

'Hail, full of grace' is from the Latin *Ave, gratia plena*. Luke's melodious Greek is *Chaire kecharitomene*. *Chaire* literally means 'rejoice'. But it was also a word of greeting and this sense was accepted in the Latin *Ave* and in various vernacular versions. *Kecharitomene* means 'highly favoured, engraced, blessed (by God)'. 'The Lord is with thee': another expression of God's loving choice of Mary for a unique role in the communication of divine life to the world. 'Blessed art thou among women' is Elizabeth's version of Gabriel's 'kecharitomene'. 'Blessed is the fruit of thy womb': Elizabeth goes to the human heart of the matter and gives Jesus a description that fits every child: an invitation here to contemplate the Lord's humanity and Mary's motherhood and to remember all children, especially those at risk.

The first part of the Hail Mary came into liturgical use in the ancient Church both in east and west. The second text given here is from ancient eastern liturgy. An almost verbatim version of it is still used in the Orthodox Church.

In the medieval period, through the Little Office of Our Lady and the Rosary, the first part of the Hail Mary became a prayer of the people. Bishops directed that the people should know it along with the Our Father and the Creed. The Holy Name was added by direction, it is thought, of Pope Urban IV (1261-1264).

The Holy Mary part of the prayer was a later development but it had certainly reached its present form by, say, 1500. It completes the praise of Our Lady with the greatest of her titles and expresses her children's need of her and trust in her.

5. IN PRAISE OF OUR LADY

1. Hail Mary, full of grace. The Lord is with thee.
   Blessed art thou among women
   and blessed is the fruit of thy womb, Jesus.
   Holy Mary, Mother of God, pray for us sinners
   now and at the hour of our death. Amen.

2. Hail/rejoice (*Chaire*) Mary, full of grace
   (*kecharitomene*), the Lord is with thee.
   Blessed art thou among women
   and blessed is the fruit of thy womb
   because you conceived Christ
   the Son of God, the Saviour of our souls.

1. 'We fly to your protection' honours Our Lady as
Theotokos (God-bearer, Mother of God). It can be traced
back to a Greek script of a century or so before the
Council of Ephesus (431) which officially proclaimed the
title while treating of the Incarnation of the Lord. Let us
cherish this remarkable prayer that links us with the early
Church.

2-4. This greatest of Marian titles is very characteristic
of Orthodox prayers to Our Lady. Three are given here:
'Unfailing Protector' (which resembles 'We fly to your
protection'), the morning and evening outpouring of
praise 'It is entirely right' and an antiphon from the
Byzantine Book of Hours.

1. We fly to your protection, O holy Mother of God:
    do not despise our prayers in our necessities
    but free us from all dangers,
    O glorious and blessed Virgin.

2. Unfailing Protector of Christians, unfailing
    advocate with the Creator, do not despise the appeals
    of sinners but graciously be prompt to help us who
    call on you in faith. Mother of God, constant defender
    of your suppliants, be swift to hear our prayer.

3. It is entirely right to call you blessed
    you who gave birth to God
    ever blessed and most innocent
    the Mother of our God
    We praise and extol you, true Mother of God
    more worthy of honour than the cherubim
    greater in glory than the seraphim
    the sinless bearer of the Eternal Word

4. Rejoice, full of grace!
    God-bearer and pure Virgin!
    From you has come the Sun of justice, Christ our God,
    the Light of those in darkness!

1. The beautiful *Salve Regina* was probably written by the remarkable Hermann the Cripple (1013-1054), Benedictine monk of Reichenau in Switzerland, deformed in body, brilliant in mind, lovable in character. He probably wrote the music too – though not the haunting melody we usually hear.

Various religious orders, led by the Cistercians, put it into their liturgies. The laity liked it too and it became a favourite of sailors. Christopher Columbus wrote in his logbook on 11 October 1492: 'When they said the *Salve* which all the sailors are in the habit of saying and singing in their way … the Admiral … admonished the men … to keep a good lookout for land.' The next day they sighted America.

A *Salve* evening service for the laity developed and this led to evening Benediction of the Blessed Sacrament. Perhaps the eucharistic 'showing' was thought of as a kind of anticipation of the overwhelming 'showing' that we ask Our Lady for in this prayer. As indeed it is.

2. The *Memorare* (Remember) is often credited to Saint Bernard of Clairvaux (1090-1153) but the evidence is not convincing.Another Bernard is definitely associated with it: Claude Bernard (1588-1641), a zealous priest of Paris who worked for prisoners and those sentenced to death. This prayer was his great expression of confidence in Our Lady and he promoted it tirelessly. With the exception perhaps of the last sentence ('O Mother of the Word Incarnate …') it was actually part of a much longer prayer which can be traced back to an early printed work of 1489. It echoes the 'protection' prayer of the early Church. There is a very similar prayer addressed to Our Lady of Peace.

1. Hail, holy Queen, Mother of mercy.
   Hail, our life, our sweetness and our hope.
   To thee do we cry, poor banished children of Eve.
   To thee do we send up our sighs,
   mourning and weeping in this valley of tears.
   Turn then, most gracious Advocate,
   thine eyes of mercy towards us
   and after this our exile show unto us
   the blessed fruit of thy womb, Jesus.
   O clement, O loving, O sweet Virgin Mary.

2. Remember, O most gracious Virgin Mary,
   that never was it known
   that anyone who fled to thy protection,
   implored thy help or sought thy intercession
   was left unaided.
   Inspired by this confidence, I fly unto thee,
   O Virgin of virgins, my Mother:
   to thee do I come, before thee I stand
   sinful and sorrowful.
   O Mother of the Word Incarnate,
   despise not my petitions but, in thy clemency,
   hear and answer me.
   Amen.

1-2. Augustine of Hippo Regius (354-430) is one of the greatest intellects in the history of the Church and became the dominant theological influence in the western Church for many centuries. He has been called 'Doctor of the West'. Because of his emphasis on God's grace he is also 'Doctor of Grace'. His *Confessions* is the most famous and influential of Christian autobiographies. It is really an extended prayer, interspersed with lyrical upliftings of the heart to God, two of which are given here.

3. Bede (c. 673-735), Benedictine monk of Jarrow on Tyneside, was the intellectual star of the early English Church. He is chiefly famous for his *Ecclesiastical History of the English People,* the first major work to use an A(nno) D(omini) dating. He delighted in his teaching and writing. His pupil Cuthbert gives a moving account of the close of his life until the moment when 'chanting "Glory be to the Father and to the Son and to the Holy Spirit", when he had named the Holy Spirit, he breathed his last.'

4-5. From Scotland comes praise of Our Lady in a Latin hymn by the eighth-century Cúcuimhne, monk of Iona. From Ireland comes a strongly scriptural prayer by the eleventh-century Maol Íosa Ó Brolcháin.

6. SIGNED PRAYERS AND LAST PRAYERS

1. You have made us for yourself
    and our heart is restless until it rests in you.

2. ** Late have I loved you, beauty so old and so new,
    late have I loved you! And indeed you were within
    and I was without and there I sought you and rushed,
    unbeautiful, after those beautiful things you have
    made. You were with me and I was not with you.
    Things held me far from you: things which, if they
    were not in you, would not be at all. You called and
    shouted and penetrated my deafness. You flashed
    and shone and put my blindness to flight. You wafted
    your perfume and I breathed in and I pant for you.
    I tasted and I hunger and thirst. You touched me
    and I went on fire for your peace.

3. Glory be to the Father and to the Son
    and to the Holy Spirit.

4. Mother of the Lord, she brought the cure we needed
    for our ills
    greatest holy Virgin, steadfast in her love, beyond
    compare
    she conceived the Pearl for whom good Christians
    give up everything

5. ** Dear Christ, may the Spirit swiftly come to us,
    surround us, be in us.

The much-loved Saint Francis of Assisi (1182-1226), who has inspired so many to follow Christ in joy and simplicity of life, saw the things of nature as gifts of God. When he was very ill and near to death he composed his *Canticle of the Sun*. It has been called the first great poem in Italian. It is a prayer for our own time to help us to appreciate our God-given and threatened environment.

Be praised, my Lord, in all your creatures
and in the first place Brother Sun
He makes the day-time: through him you give light
and he is radiant, beautiful, bright
his glory tells of you
Be praised, my Lord, in all your creatures
be praised for Sister Moon and stars
for Brother Wind and the air and the clouds
for all the seasons that bring us our food
be praised, my Lord, be praised
For Sister Water, serving in purity
for blazing Brother Fire, swift in his energy
be praised for Sister-Mother Earth
she keeps and feeds us and nurses the roots
she gives the plants and the flowers and the fruits
be praised, my Lord, be praised
For all who pardon and are patient
for ever-present Sister Death
but woe to those whom she'll find in their sin
but joy to those whom she'll find in your will
O bless and serve him in joyful humility
be praised, my Lord, be praised

Catherine Benincasa (c.1347-1380) is the most famous citizen in the history of Siena. This dyer's daughter and member of the Dominican Third Order became a mystic and the spiritual mother of a varied family of laity, priests and religious. She was at least partly responsible for the return of Pope Gregory XI to Rome from Avignon and spent the last eighteen months of her life trying to restore unity to the Church sundered by rival claimants to the papacy.

1. In 1378 she wrote her *Dialogue,* her spiritual testament in which she offered her life 'as a sacrifice for the mystical Body of Holy Church'. The excerpt from the *Dialogue* given here echoes Augustine.

2. Joan of Arc is the most famous woman in the history of France. This young peasant woman, who helped to saved the French monarchy and state, was executed at the age of nineteen by burning for heresy in Rouen in 1431 by an unholy alliance of local church authority and power-politics. Her last prayer through the flames and smoke was the repeated Holy Name.

1.** Eternal Trinity: you are the Creator and I am the
creature. And you have enlightened me to know
that in your re-making of me through the blood of
your only-begotten Son you fell in love with the
beauty of what you had made...

In the mirror of this light I know you the supreme
good, the good beyond all good ... the beauty
beyond all beauty, the wisdom beyond all wisdom
... You feast us who are famished on your sweetness
because you are sweet without any bitterness, eternal
Trinity!

2. Jesu!

1. Ignatius Loyola (1491-1556), founder of the Society of Jesus, expressed his pattern of personal following of Christ in his *Spiritual Exercises*. 'Take and receive' is the prayer in the 'Contemplation for obtaining love' which sees God as infinite goodness, the ultimate source of all created good.

2. Thomas More (1477/78-1535) was a legal light in the England of his time and one of the foremost scholars in Europe. He became the friend and Lord Chancellor of Henry VIII but could not in conscience accept Henry's rejection of his wife and re-marriage and his claim to be under Christ the head of the Church in his realm. He was found guilty of denying that claim and was executed as a traitor.

'Give me thy grace' is from a long prayer written in the Tower of London before his trial. It is a good example of strong pre-Shakespearean modern English.

3. Some years after More's death, Thomas Cranmer (1489-1556), first Anglican Archbishop of Canterbury who also died for his beliefs, began to create an Anglican liturgy in English. Given here is his stylish collect for the first Sunday of Advent.

4. John of the Cross (c. 1542-1591), friend of Teresa of Avila and like her a great Carmelite and mystic, loved to pray out-of-doors, especially at night; but he wrote most of his *Spiritual Canticle* in a prison cell in Toledo. 'Seeking my Love' is an excerpt from that work which is both a celebration of God as the utterly Beautiful and Desirable and a masterpiece of Spanish literature.

1. Take, Lord, and receive all my liberty, my memory, my understanding and all my will, all that I have and possess. You have given it to me: to you, Lord, I return it; all is yours: dispose of it entirely as you will. Give me your love and grace for that is enough for me.

2. Give me your grace, good Lord, to set the world at naught, to set my mind fast upon thee and not to hang upon the blast of men's mouths.

3. Almighty God, give us grace that we may cast away the works of darkness, and put upon us the armour of light, now in the time of this mortal life (in the which thy Son Jesus Christ came to visit us in great humility) that in the last day, when he shall come again in his glorious Majesty, to judge both the quick and the dead, we may rise to the life immortal, through him who liveth and reigneth with thee and the Holy Ghost, now and forever. Amen.

4. Seeking my Love
   I'll travel the mountains and strands …
   silver-clear fount
   be a mirror of longed-for eyes.

George Herbert (1593-1633), one of the 'Metaphysical' poets, wrote no secular verse. His poetry is personalised and prayerful. In his last years he was an ordained minister of the Church of England. On the Sunday before his death he rose from his sick-bed and praised God with viol and lute in the lines presented here.

2-3. In seventeenth-century Ireland Seán Ó Conaill turned to Our Lady at the end of his 'Lament for Ireland' after the Cromwellian catastrophe. Another client of hers was the eighteenth-century poet Tadhg Gaelach Ó Súilleabháin who almost certainly was the author of the most celebrated expression in Irish of devotion to the Heart of Christ: *Gile mo chroí do Chroíse, a Shlánaitheoir* (Saviour, your Heart is the radiance of mine). The first stanza and envoi are given here.

4. From the Methodist tradition comes an excerpt from 'Morning Hymn' by Charles Wesley (d. 1788), the great writer of hymns (he is said to have written over six thousand!) of that famous evangelical movement and brother of John, its founder.

1. My God, my God,
   my music shall find thee
   and every string
   shall have his attribute to sing.

   ⌘

2. Hail Mary, full of grace
   blessed are you, the Lord is with you.
   Pray for us, friend, when we're disturbed
   now and always and you'll be heard

   ⌘

3.** Dear Lord, your Heart is the radiance of my own,
   my heart delights that yours is so near to me.
   Clearly your Heart keeps loving me utterly
   so make your Heart a shield for my heart deep-down.

   You came from heaven, you walked on human shore,
   in mystery you suffered for all our sin,
   guiding in love the lance that allowed us in
   and made your Heart our dwelling forevermore.

   ⌘

4. Christ, whose glory fills the skies,
   Christ the true, the only light,
   Sun of Righteousness, arise!
   Triumph o'er the shades of night!
   Day-spring from on high, be near!
   Day-star, in my heart appear!

1. John Henry Newman (1801-1890) was an Anglican for the first half of his life and a Catholic for the second half and had a profound influence on both communions. He wrote 'Lead, Kindly Light' in 1833 while convalescing after a mentally disturbing illness. He was a leading light in the 'Oxford Movement' which challenged the Anglican Church establishment with a Catholicising interpretation of Anglican doctrine. He became a Catholic in 1845 and subsequently an Oratorian and cardinal. In his emphasis on the role of the laity in the Church (including their education in the faith) he foreshadowed Vatican II – which has been called 'Newman's Council'.

2-3. 'Praise to the Holiest' is from 'The Dream of Gerontius', his epic poem about the soul crossing the frontier of death, afterwards set to superb music by Elgar. The prayer for a happy death is familiar to us from memorial cards. Apart from its rich content, it is a fine example of Newman's 'cloistral' style. He had a sensitive respect for words, including words in prayer. It is said that he prayed with pen in hand.

1. Lead, kindly Light, amid the encircling gloom
   lead Thou me on
   The night is dark and I am far from home
   lead Thou me on
   Keep Thou my feet; I do not ask to see
   the distant scene – one step enough for me

   I was not ever thus, nor prayed that Thou
   shouldst lead me on
   I loved to choose and see my path; but now
   lead Thou me on
   I loved the garish day, and spite of fears
   pride ruled my will: remember not past years

   So long thy power hath blest me, since it still
   will lead me on
   o'er moor and fen, o'er crag and torrent, till
   the night is gone
   And with the morn those angel faces smile
   which I have loved long since, and lost awhile

   ∞

2. Praise to the Holiest in the heights
   and in the depths be praise,
   in all his words most wonderful,
   most sure in all his ways.

   ∞

3. My he support us all the day long till the shades
   lengthen and the evening comes and the busy world
   is hushed and the fever of life is over and our work
   is done: then in his mercy may he give us a safe
   lodging and a holy rest and peace at the last.

1. Towards the end of her short life (1873-1897), Thérèse Martin of the Lisieux Carmel wrote her autobiography which was to have an immense impact on countless Christians with its message of 'the little way' of day-to-day confidence in and surrender to God. This 'love' prayer is from that part of her story written just a year before her death.

2. Gladys Aylward (1902-1970), a London domestic servant, dreamt of being a missionary in China but had to save up her fare to get there. She did get there – and became a legend in Christian mission history. This is her prayer.

3. Franz Jägerstätter, an Austrian peasant farmer, refused to serve in the army of the Reich in World War II because he saw it as fighting for Nazism which he abhorred as essentially anti-Christian. He quoted this prayer/hymn to Our Lady in a letter to his wife and family on 9 August 1943, the day of his execution.

4. Edel Quinn (now Venerable) is one of the greatest Christian apostles of the twentieth century as envoy of the Legion of Mary to Central and East Africa and Mauritius from 1936 to 1944. She combined incredible activity with much personal charm and deep spiritual life. She said these words as she was dying in Nairobi in 1944.

1. ** Jesus my love, at last I have found my vocation: it is love. I have indeed found my own place in the Church, the place you have given me, my God. In the heart of the Church my mother I will be love and so will be all things and my desires will become reality.

2. God, here's me and here's my Bible and my money. Use us!

3. Mary with the beloved Child, give us all your blessings.

4. Is he coming? ... Jesus, Jesus.

1. Angelo Roncalli as John xxiii (now Blessed), the Pope who convoked and inspired Vatican II, is certainly one of the most important popes of modern times. Terminally ill, he woke up in the small hours of 3 June 1963 and said these words of Peter to the risen Christ (Jn 21:15-17) twice with great emphasis. He died that evening.

2. Bauduoin of Saxe-Coburg was King of the Belgians from 1951 to 1993. He gave a wonderful example of Christian kingship. He wrote this prayer on the day he died, 31 July 1993.

1. Lord, you know that I love you.

    ∞

2. Come, Holy Spirit, and pray in me: I feel very dry and weary. Mother, it is to you that I can turn to without too much effort; in faith I shall try to place myself at your feet and remain close to you. Let it be you who will carry me in prayer … I beg of you, Jesus, give me your Peace, your Joy and the fire of your Love. And may I ask you too, Lord, to enable me to persevere in writing my journal and studying my German.

7. THE SIGN AND THE SIGNATURE

1. In the name of the Father and of the Son
   and of the Holy Spirit.

   ≈

2. O Holy God, O Holy Strong One,
   O Holy Immortal One, have mercy on us.

   ≈

3. Amen.

   ≈

1-2. We begin our prayers with the Sign of the Cross, a very ancient gesture, going back perhaps to apostolic times. A sign may have accompanied the New Testament emphasis on the Cross of Christ: 1 Cor 1:17; Gal 6:14; 1 Pet 2:24 and elsewhere. The 'length and breadth and height and depth' of Eph 3:18 may be a reference to such a sign.

Whatever about apostolic times, the sign was certainly in the Church a few generations later. Two great geniuses of the early Church, Tertullian and Origen, mention it: 'Whenever we come in or go out ... at table ... in going to rest ... we rub our foreheads with the sign of the cross ... All believers make this sign in commencing any work, especially at the beginning of prayer or of reading holy scripture.' It was said that the emperor Julian (361-362), who renounced Christianity for the old paganism which he tried to restore in the empire, would instinctively make the Sign of the Cross at certain unguarded moments.

The sign was (and is) a reminder of our consecration by and to Christ in baptism, of the engracing power of his death. It seems from Tertullian that it was originally a 'forehead' sign. The large 'body sign' (forehead, breast and shoulders) developed in the eastern part of the Church and migrated to the west where it became common in the medieval period.

In the early Church the sign was made with thumb or index finger. Then when the doctrines of the Trinity and Incarnation (Christ one Person with two natures, divine and human) came under attack, orthodox believers in the east began to use two or three fingers as an expression of their faith. Most eastern Church worshippers use thumb and two fingers as does the Pope giving blessings. One very eloquent eastern usage is joining thumb and little finger to form a circle representing the one God with the other three fingers representing the Persons. In the west under Benedictine influence the open hand finally came into use. The west finally opted for a signing from left shoulder to right while the east kept right-left.

With the sign often go words. The most ancient formulas mention only Christ. One eastern invocation (given here) is the majestic 'O Holy God …' The best-known and very ancient formula, shared by east and west, is of course, 'In the name of the Father …' which comes from the great mandate at the end of the gospel of Matthew. Through it and 'O Holy God' the sign becomes the sign of the Trinity as well, of the One and the Three, of the eternal Love that broke into time in the life, death and resurrection of the Son made one of us.

When we make or accept this sign we are part of a mainstream tradition, a long pilgrimage, an immense company. We are of an ancestry that put it into its church design, its door-panelling, its daily prayers. This sign is a profession of faith, an acceptance of God's love for us in Christ. It is a salute to the God who has, we may say, put it into nature itself: trees in winter, birds in flight and the shape of ourselves.

3. We end our prayers with Amen. This is a Hebrew word meaning 'firm, true, trustworthy'. It connotes certainty and safety: the experience of the child close to the mother; even the sound of it, said softly, is like the contented murmur of a child at the breast.

The word expresses agreement with, assent to, approval of a proposal, statement. truth. It says Yes. It is, as it were, a signature: 'To say Amen', said Saint Augustine, 'is to sign your name.'

The ultimate truth we say Amen to is God. For Christians it is Yes to God as revealed in the Christ-event. The word is frequent in this sense in the New Testament. Jesus himself uses it to emphasise specially important statements. In the epistles it often concludes petitions and praise-statements. The Book of Revelation, the last book of the New Testament, says that Amen is sung in heaven, and ends with Amen on a note of longing for the definitive coming of Christ. Saint Paul says, 'All the promises of God find their Yes in him (Christ). That is why we utter the Amen through him to the glory of God' (2 Cor 1:20)

He may be referring here to the most important

Amen in the public life of the Church: that at the end of the Eucharistic Prayer in the Mass. It expresses our Yes to the plan of God in Christ concentrated in the Eucharist in our daily life. Let us join in it from our hearts. Let us make our whole life an Amen unto and into the eternal glory and joy. Amen. Amen. Amen.

APPENDIX

Musical Settings

All of these settings, except that for *Deeply I Adore You,*
are by Stephen Redmond SJ.

Lead, Kindly Light

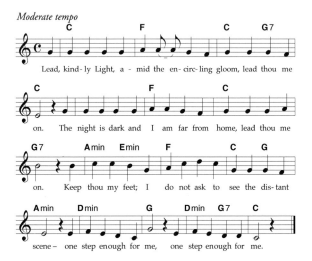

Moderate tempo

Lead, kind-ly Light, a - mid the en-circ-ling gloom, lead thou me on. The night is dark and I am far from home, lead thou me on. Keep thou my feet; I do not ask to see the dis-tant scene – one step enough for me, one step enough for me.

(This setting is in memory of my father, from whom I first learned of Newman and this poem. — *S.R.*)

The complete text is on page 85

Christis Near *(Christus venit)*

Moderate tempo

Night and the dark and clouds tu-mul-tu-ous in rout De-part! The sky is white-ning, Christ is near.

Sun-ar-rows pierce the mist and col-our's com-ing out and look! The morn-ing star is shin-ing clear.

The complete text is on page 45

The Banners of the King *(Vexilla Regis)*

Moderate tempo

The ban-ners of the King ad - vance, the
Cross is shin - ing mys - te - ry and
Life in Per - son suf - fers death, by
death gives life, makes free. A
wound - ed King, the wood his throne, a
fi - nal thrust: the lance goes in and
blood and wa - ter from his Heart to
cleanse our hearts from sin.

A longer text is on page 47

Tree of Trees *(Pange Lingua Lauream)*

Moderate tempo

Cross so faith - ful! Tree of trees, the
no - blest tree that ev - er stood,
nev - er did a for - est bear such
glor - ious flower and leaf and bud
sweet the wood and nails that bear the
sweet - est weight of flesh and blood.

A longer text is on page 49

The original Latin can be sung to this melody

Come, All in Him *(Sancti Venite)*

The complete text is on page 51

Greatest Sacrament *(Pange Lingua Mysterium)*

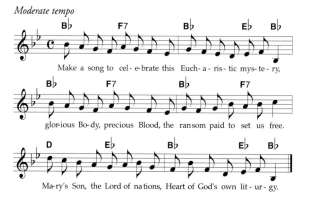

Moderate tempo

Make a song to cel - e-brate this Euch-a-ris-tic mys-te-ry,

glor-ious Bo-dy, precious Blood, the ran som paid to set us free.

Ma-ry's Son, the Lord of na tions, Heart of God's own lit-ur-gy.

The complete text is on page 55

The original Latin can be sung to this melody

Holy Banquet *(O Sacrum Convivium)*

Rather slowly

Ho - ly Ban - quet hea - ven - sent, Christ, him - self, our
nour - ish - ment, pro - claim - ing of his Pas - sion, of his
death on Cal - va - ry. Gift to fill the
heart with grace 'till we see him face to face,
prom - ise of e - ter - nal life, of fu - ture glo - ry.

The text is also on page 53

Deeply I Adore You *(Adoro Te Devote)*

Moderate tempo

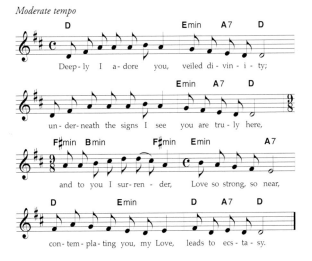

Deep-ly I a-dore you,   veiled di-vin-i-ty;

un-der-neath the signs I see   you are tru-ly here,

and to you I sur-ren-der,   Love so strong, so near,

con-tem-pla-ting you, my Love,   leads to ecs-ta-sy.

A longer text is on page 53

Heart of Grace *(Cor Arca Legem Continens)*

Moderate tempo

You are the ark   that holds the law   not of the for - mer

sla - ve - ry,   law of for - give - ness, mer - cy, grace,____

____ that sets us   free.   Heart that's the house of

cov - en - ant,   ho - ly ground here – let none de - face,

tem - ple of tem - ples, hea - ven - sent,____   the veil of

grace.   to   see your   face.

The complete text is on page 59

Radiant Heart *(Gile mo Chroí)*

Slowly

Dear Lord, your Heart is the rad-iance of my own, my heart de-lights that yours is so near to me. Clear-ly your Heart keeps lov-ing me ut-ter-ly, so make your Heart a shield for my heart deep-down.

A longer text is on page 83

Come, Creator Spirit *(Veni, Creator Spiritus)*

Moderate tempo

Come, O Cre-a-tor, Spi-rit, come, welcome to you, dear
Friend to-day. Fill all the hearts that you have made,____
____ come, Spi-rit, stay. Gift that is God and
Friend at hand, lis-ten-ing, un-der-stand-ing, freeing,
fountain a-live and fire and love,____ balm of our
being. Come, Spi-rit, come.

The complete text is on page 61

Holy Spirit *(Nunc, Sancte Spiritus)*

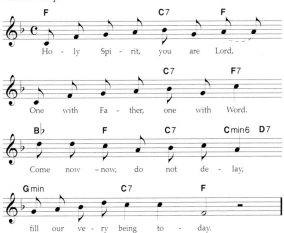

Moderate tempo

Ho - ly Spi - rit, you are Lord,
One with Fa - ther, one with Word.
Come now - now, do not de - lay,
fill our ve - ry being to - day.

The complete text is on page 63

Hail, Holy Queen *(Salve Regina)*

Rather slowly

Hail, ho - ly Queen, Mo - ther of mer - cy,
our life, our sweet-ness and our hope, – hail ho - ly Queen.
To you we cry, poor ban-ished child-ren of Eve,
to you we sigh and mourn and weep in this val - ley of
tears. Turn towards us, Ad - vo-cate, your eyes of
mer - cy, and af - ter ex - ile, show us your Je - sus.
O clem - ent, lov - ing, sweet Vir - gin Ma - ry,
show us the fruit of your womb, Je - sus.

The text is taken almost verbatim from that on page 73

God-bearer *(Theotokos)*

Rather slowly

Chai-re, hail, re-joice! The-ot-o-kos, God-bearer, pur-est one. From your womb has come the Lord who ends the night and makes us free. Christ the Light of all in dark-ness, Sun of free-dom, Christ our God.

Mother of the Lord, you brought the cure
   we needed for our ills
Virgin, holy one, so steadfast in your love
   beyond compare
you conceived the Pearl for whom
   good Christians give up everything

The words are a paraphrase of the texts on pages 69 and 75